73

New Shoes on a Dead Horse
a collection of poetry

℘

by Sierra DeMulder

Write Bloody Publishing
America's Independent Press

Long Beach, CA

WRITEBLOODY.COM

DeMulder, Sierra.
1ˢᵗ edition.
ISBN: 978-1-935904-95-3

Interior Layout by Lea C. Deschenes
Cover Designed by Matt Maust
Proofread by Jennifer Roach, Stevie Edwards, and Sarah Kay
Edited by Jamie Garbacik, Courtney Olsen, Alexis Davis, Sarah Kay, Dylan Garity, Gabrielle Dunkley, and Derrick Brown
Type set in Bergamo from www.theleagueofmoveabletype.com

Printed in Tennessee, USA

Write Bloody Publishing
Long Beach, CA
Support Independent Presses
writebloody.com

To contact the author, send an email to writebloody@gmail.com

This book is dedicated to my parents.

New Shoes on a Dead Horse

The Romans did not actually think that a genius was a particularly clever individual. They believed that a genius was this sort of magical divine entity who [lived] in the walls of an artist's studio [and] would come out and invisibly assist the artist with their work.
—Elizabeth Gilbert

Ah that our Genius were a little more of a genius!
—Ralph Waldo Emerson

A poem is a naked person.
—Bob Dylan

New Shoes on a Dead Horse

IV

I

THE GENIUS AND THE SOUP KITCHEN

On opening day, no one showed up.
Same with the next. And the next.
And the next.

Finally, he unplugged the Open sign.
He waited for it to cool before bending
the letters, forming new words
with electric yarn.

You Will Find Everything Here
now glows in the window. At first,
only a few questions crawled
through the door. Soon, unfinished

sentences. Eventually, herds
of priests, atheists, whole families of
extinct animals.

Today, there is a four hour wait
just to stand inside. Starving,

they ask about winning
lottery numbers, lost family
recipes, the necessity of exercise.
Is there a God? Why doesn't he return

my phone calls? Where did I leave
my car keys? When a tree falls
in the forest, does it suffer?

He serves bowls of bubbling
Compliments. Slices of Financial Advice.
Entire legs of Answers, fresh cut
Answers, baked Answers served
with butter and garlic.

When they leave, he hears them
use words like full, content.

He has stopped sleeping at night.
He lies in bed and watches the hours
clock in and out of their shifts.

I am a dumb doctor.
A Novocain prescription.
I am new shoes
on a dead horse.

THE PERM

The first time my mother stood up
to my father, she got her hair permed.
He had told her not to—said it was
a waste of my hard-earned money.

My father tells me this story while crying.
He is softer now, a treadless tire.
My mother came home from the salon,
and I'll be damned, Sierra, if it didn't look
terrible. It killed me, I swear to God.

This perm, the first mutter
in a soundless room, the swing of the bat
only to find the piñata is a real dog.

Now, thirty years later, I am a poet
and I am telling this story as if it were mine.
I am harvesting this splinter.
This embarrassing toothache.

I am dragging my father's temper out of storage
by the wrist. I am making my mother drive home
from the salon over and over and over.

THE ORIGIN OF BREAST MILK

It began after the rape of St. Agatha,
a woman of God imprisoned in a brothel
for a month for rejecting a suitor.

She did not cry, even as
the shade was drawn on the first night
and the worst, most tired
parts of men found
themselves at her bedroom door.

Her first lover was a boy,
no older than fourteen.
Her second, a blacksmith.
Her third tasted like wet stone
and looked like her brother.
Her fourth, a drunkard, a widower.

In the morning, while Agatha slept,
women throughout Sicily
suddenly dropped their baskets of fruit
and pots of boiling water, their hands
grasping their chests—a wetness,

spilling, soaking through
every blouse. The doctors were called,
even the midwives. Women
began fastening cloth
around their torsos with twine.

Months later, months after
Agatha's breasts were cut off,
one woman weary with a colicky babe
untied the twine, pushed
the angry mouth to her nipple.

The child coughed at first,
then quieted, and it was all
so familiar. It was the way
it had always been but gentler,
the taking, the giving.

ON WATCHING SOMEONE YOU LOVE LOVE SOMEONE ELSE

You will be out with friends when the news of her existence is accidentally spilled all over your bar stool. Respond calmly as if it was only a change in weather, a punch line you saw coming. After your fourth shot of cheap liquor, leave the image of him kissing another woman in the toilet.

In the morning, her name will be in every headline: Car Crash, Robbery, Flood. When he calls you, ignore the hundreds of ropes untangling themselves in your stomach; you are the best friend again. When he invites you over for dinner, say yes too easily. Remind yourself: this isn't special. It's only dinner. Everyone has to eat. When he greets you at the door, do not think for one second you are the reason he wore cologne tonight.

In his kitchen, he will hand-feed you a piece of red pepper. His laugh will be low and warm and it will make you feel like candlelight. Do not think this is special. Do not count on your fingers the freckles you could kiss too easily. Try to think of pilot lights or olive oil, not everything you have ever loved about him, or it will suddenly feel boiling and possible and so close.

You will find her bobby pins lying innocently on his bathroom sink. Her bobby pins. They look like the wiry legs of spiders, splinters of her undressing in his bed. Do not say anything. Think of stealing them, wearing them home in your hair. When he hugs you goodbye, let him kiss you on the forehead. Settle for target practice.

At home, you will picture her across town, pressing her fingers into his back like wet cement. You will wonder if she looks like you, if you are two bedrooms in the same house. Did he fall for her features like rearranged furniture? When he kisses her, does she taste like new paint?

You will want to call him. You will go as far as holding the phone in your hand, imagine telling him unimaginable things like—*You are always ticking inside of me and I dream of you more often than I don't. My body is a dead language and you pronounce each word perfectly.* Do not call him. Fall asleep to the hum of the VCR. She must make him happy. She must be—she must be his favorite place in Minneapolis. You are a souvenir shop, where he goes to remember how much people miss him when he is gone.

THE GENIUS GOES TO THE ART MUSEUM

He enjoys the entrance the most, but not because of the gift shop. He already owns hundreds of magnets and an impressive coffee mug collection that crowds his counters and windowsills. He started collecting mugs to hold his other collections: pennies dated before 1943, capless markers, lithium batteries, hundreds of marker caps. He is particularly proud of his denture collection, which he found makes an adequate calendar. Every morning after breakfast, but before shaving, he retrieves his current pair. Before fitting the smile into his mouth, he pulls out one tooth per day. Plastic gums, like pink half-eaten sandwiches cover his bathroom floor. Each with only one or two teeth left, depending on the month. Today, he has seventeen teeth. He is sitting on a bench outside the coat check at the art museum and does not intend to go any farther. It is not that he doesn't enjoy art. He believes it is just like masturbating. *Sometimes you have to do it and sometimes you just do it because you're bored.* He even paints occasionally, but not as much as the other thing. He visits the art museum every 8th tooth not to look at beautiful things but to watch beautiful things come and go. A toddler drawing a koi fish in the air with his finger. A purple-haired teenager pickled in angst humming a tune she has never heard before. A woman searching for a pen. An old man who cannot stop crying. He is watching art in its purest form. The moment of inception. The shaken soda can. The blister.

YOUR SON HAS A BEAUTIFUL VOICE
After Sharon Olds

Once, outside of an ice cream shop,
he told me of how you got sick.
How he was ten years old and how
he used to fall asleep in the backseat
during the long drive up north
to the better hospital. How he knew
the end was near because that week,
the preacher spoke of how God giveth
and especially of how God taketh away.
How he woke up in the middle of that night,
in the middle of a dream, and walked into
your room. How you passed right then,
as if waiting for his permission to teach him
all that you could about life. How the crying
seemed to go on forever. How suddenly,
one day, it stopped and how he has not
cried since. I fall asleep beside him now,
listening to the way his breath untangles
itself from the day, like you must have
when he was small or still do. He speaks
of you, but with the delicacy of recalling
a dream: not dwelling too long on the details,
as if fearful the memory might fade completely.
Your son has a beautiful voice. I am afraid
I love him enough to listen to it forever.
I am afraid he loves me enough to cry if I leave.

THE ORIGIN OF THE BATHROBE

Queen Mary stopped bathing
after her first miscarriage. She refused
to change her bedding, damp
with the wetness of labor and loss.

It was a compromise, at least,
to air them out to dry. They hung
like huge watercolor paintings on the trees,
plumes of sweat, blood, the spill
of what did not come.

By her seventh, the chambermaids
began wrapping scented scarves
around their faces. The Queen's nightgown
now stuck to her belly and thighs,
stiff, more red than white.
She seemed always pregnant

and always not. The ladies-in-waiting
were not foolish. They understood.
If a man were to see the Queen, soiled,
pacing ghostlike, no woman

would wear the crown again.
The ladies pulled down the curtains
and bed canopy and measured their bodies
by lying like dead angels on the floor.

Twelve matching housecoats
adorned with pillow tassels
and petticoat lace. Twelve
matching housecoats strolling
through the garden. Under one,
a tapestry of grief.

Beginning with an Orgasm and Ending in Slaughter
After Kim Addonizio

The moment he made my body
pulse like the crack of opening
a soda can, I thought of her: the woman
who climbed out from the cellar

of his infidelity. Her face came to me
as if our sex had summoned her, as if I had
been calling her name the whole time,
warning the town of her approach. Behold!

She will come at nightfall.
She will ride a carriage pulled behind
two drowned horses. She will set fire to
the houses. She will slaughter all the calves.

She will slide her bloody shadow
into my lover's bed to sleep, as bright
and shivering as a newborn
babe, between us.

THE GENIUS VISITS THE PSYCHIC

He went to see her not because he really needed to
know something, but because he once sat next to her
in a bar and drunkenly put his hand on the counter
next to her hand and she did not slap it away

or stab him. He also heard a rumor she worked
part-time as a stripper downtown. She charged him double
and smoked vinegary cigarettes in the walk-in closet
where she read tabloids of the future. YOU

WILL TRIP OVER A BANANA PEEL AND INTO
A GARBAGE CAN OF MONEY was one she was
known for. She dug her acrylic nails into the meat
of his palm as if scratching a coin for copper.
SHE WILL FIND LOVE. *Good one, very original.*
SHE WILL FIND HAPPINESS. *I know,*
I know. Now get to the good stuff.

I wanna know about heartbreak.
Show me the lies. Tell me
the tears are coming, those wet
necklaces, those pretty little thorns.

LOVE, FORGIVE ME
After Rachel McKibbens

My sister told me a soul mate is not the person
who makes you the happiest, but the one who
makes you feel the most. Who conducts your heart

to bang the loudest. Who can drag you giggling
with forgiveness from the cellar they locked you in.
It has always been you. You are the first

person I was afraid to sleep next to,
not because of the fear you would leave
in the night but because I didn't want to wake up

gracelessly. In the morning, I crawled over
your lumbering chest to wash my face and pinch
my cheeks and lay myself out like a still-life

beside you. Your new girlfriend is pretty
like the cover of a cookbook. I have said her name
into the empty belly of my apartment. Forgive me.

When I feel myself falling out of love
with you, I turn the record of your laughter
over, reposition the needle.

I have imagined our children. Forgive me. I made up
the best parts of you. Forgive me. When you told me
to look for you on my wedding day, to pause

on the altar for the sound of your voice
before sinking myself into the pond of another
love, forgive me. I mistook it for a promise.

II

COLOR

In second grade, I sit next to Preston
because his name starts with P
and my name starts with S and no one
in our class has a Q or R name.

His skin reminds me of the wet sand
in my driveway, like a birthmark
spilled all over his body.

My grandmother told me I have a birthmark
because an angel kissed the inside of my elbow.
I watch Preston color his name tag
and imagine an angel
swallowing him whole.

One day, our teacher does not come to school
and the principal tells us her skin is sick
and the doctor will cut off the bad parts.

That day, we paint construction paper
to send to the hospital. Someone asks Preston
if he is dirty or sick. I spill brown
down the front of my dress and
cry in the bathroom. That day, Preston
is picked last in gym class,
after the boy in the cast.

The New Kitchen

After the divorce, my mother moved
out of the house my father built from lumber
he cut and stripped and varnished. She bought

different furniture. She framed
all the photographs. Her new kitchen

is small. The plastic cupboards
are painted to look like wood grain
and the counter is a shade of red

only found in nature. The dishes match—
something I can tell comforts my mother,
the woman who wore flowers in her hair

on her wedding day. Who can charm
bread to rise. Who taught me
when to pick a tomato off the vine.

I still find old parts of her lying
around the house. Frayed scraps
of quilting fabric. Mismatched silverware.

For a while, I imagined
what would have become of her
if she had stayed with my father
at the top of that hill

with the wood stove smoke
and the swinging screen door,
how fast she might have wilted.

I have one memory of her
in the old kitchen. She is standing
at the stained sink and I am not tall enough

to see over the counter. She is crying
as she plucks the feathers
from a sleeping chicken.

Sometimes, I whitewash
this image. I choose not to
remember the smell.

In this one, the bird is bathing in the sink.
In this one, she still has flowers in her hair.

THE GENIUS COMPLAINS ABOUT HIS BOSS

She just sits there at a fucking coffee shop
(*real* original) and somehow it's my fault
she doesn't write The Poem.

I have my own life, you know. I've got kids
at home. I've got things to do. She doesn't
care. It's not my fault she's cooking or having

sex or driving and she can't stop to write it
down. Shit, girl doesn't even know
what makes her tick. I swear, she edits her diary.

DEAR DIARY,

I AM ~~SO DEPRESSED~~ DROWNING
IN AN ~~ENORMOUS~~ ENDLESS POOL OF MISERY.
I ~~LOVE DO NOT LOVE~~ DON'T CARE
ABOUT ~~HIM HIM HIM~~ ANYTHING ANYMORE.
ALSO, ~~MY MOM SENT ME A CUTE BIRTHDAY CARD~~
I AM ALONE.

How's she gonna write a poem without me, huh?
What's it gonna be about? Flowers? Sadness?
Good luck. Good fucking luck.

Baptism

The twins who found the dead body in the river
stopped coming to school the last week of fifth grade.
We rode our bicycles to the payphone,

dialed their number, swore we smelled their mother's cigarette
smoke through the receiver. They never came out. By July,
they were a ghost story we told the younger children—

how the river swallowed their voices, dulled
their eyes into four dry stones. All summer,
we swam in pools, savored the clear chlorine.

The twins returned for the first day of sixth grade
in matching silk blouses. Their breasts had unwrapped
themselves from under their skin. Their legs no longer

childish planks. We tried not to stare, to whisper.
They sat alone at lunch and we gossiped about what happens
to girls who look like women. That night, one by one,

we snuck out of our homes, unplanned, to swim naked
in the river. To baptize the closed rosebuds of our nipples.
To float amongst corpses. To drown the child in us.

GIRL
After Jamaica Kincaid

This is how you bend over in the front row of the classroom so he can see your thong. This is how to know the answer but not raise your hand. This is how to giggle like a dinner bell. No, not like the emptying of a gutter. Like a dinner bell, like you better come in before it gets dark. Better make him walk you home. This is how to make jokes about your breasts. This is how to make cleavage outta small tits. This is how to spill into his lap like a plush blanket. This is how to expect him to rip off your dress. When he doesn't, this is how to do it for him. This is how to press and squeeze his hand against your nipple. I don't care if you feel nothing. Don't tell him you feel nothing or you'll walk home alone in the dark. This is how you moan. This is how you say Yes. I don't care if you feel nothing. Spit in your hand. Pretend to be wet.

THE GENIUS PONDERS HIS MUSE

He spends 4 hours in the delivery room.
The poem comes out, as they always do,
dressed in black, always on the way

to another funeral. His friends
and family rush to the hospital
with bouquets of pink and blue

balloons and an oversized teddy bear,
Proud Father sewn into its stomach.
After hearing the poem, after holding it

swaddled in their mouths, they leave heavier
than before, some crying, some shredding
bits of paper in their coat pockets.

———

"Why are they always *so* sad?"
his mother finally complained
at the Thanksgiving dinner table.

———

Was it the Elliott Smith song
or, maybe, the coffee mug that dropped
on the carpet? How beautiful it was

that it did not shatter
but bounced. Perhaps because the clock
on his stove runs 4 minutes fast

which makes him feel like even time
doesn't want to be with him.
Sadness is the bathrobe he wears

when he is expecting company.
It is his eldest brother. It has been there
as far back as he can remember.

THE GENIUS SHARES HIS OPINION OF ASTROLOGY

And you know what else? She's all proud
to be a Gemini. She tells everyone,

as if crazy was a prize
show horse she wants to tie up

in the front yard. Why would anyone
want to feel things twice?

Like *yes, I'll take the electric chair*
and the spear. I'll have the food poisoning

and the arsenic. May I please fall in love with
two different people at the same time until

love is peeling itself away from me
in all directions like I am a fucking banana

or a wishbone. Some days,
I feel sorry for her. I really do.

She doesn't realize it, but she is starving.
She's got too many mouths to feed

on that head of hers. She's got
too many heads on that vase of a neck.

Must be like making love
to a puppet show.

FENTANYL

I

At night, you took pills that costumed death
in a warm summer dress.

It was only then that you would reach for me,

so I took my share like a Pavlovian dog
and we fucked like floating in dishwater.

II

You asked me not to write about this.

III

Numbness did not exit your body
quietly. It clawed at the tiles

as it was dragged out. Trying so hard

to hand-feed the rabid, I did not understand
the nature of withdrawal. I would ignore

your foaming mouth, let you suckle a sleeping pill

or nipple, my body a worthless anesthetic.
I dreamt of snarling dogs, a dried worm on the sidewalk,

a mother nursing limp, blue lips.

THE GENIUS PERFORMS TAXIDERMY

He did minimal research.
He fell asleep reading *How To
Stuff The Dead* and dreamed of a child
throwing up forever and did not read anymore.

He knew it must be dry, so he hung it

like laundry from the pipes.
He knew to remove handfuls of it,
fists of slugs, the stomach of a pumpkin.

His workspace was not ideal.
There was sawdust on the floor. The light
was yellow and tired. The whole room
looked seasick. He heaved

the Love onto the butcher's block,
lifted its limp neck. He knew from the sloppy
twine stitches and the mismatched eyebrows that

this was not its first time dying. The eyes

were taped open. The mouth was agape,
drooling strands of hay. The skin like a pillowcase
stuffed with newspaper. *This poor beast*

he thought as he threaded
the needle with fishing line.

III

WAKE UP

2005 — A girl is born with four arms and four legs. She resembles the multi-limbed Hindu goddess Lakshmi, who is worshiped as a deity of wealth and good fortune. The baby is named after the goddess and revered throughout India as the reincarnation.

2007 — 2-year-old Lakshmi survives an extensive surgery to remove her "parasitic twin" that stopped developing in her mother's womb.

I am waking up.
I am waking up wrapped
like a new cut from the butcher.

I am the flower and the bulb.
I am the tree and the reflection
of the tree in the river. Wake up

reflection. Wake up shadow.
Make me a sea creature
or a Rorschach painting.

Make me a temple. Wake up
foundation. Wake up sleepyhead.
It's time to dance. It's time to hold—

to do what humans do best.
Some sleep through it, when the gold
yolk pours from the crack

in the sky. I am here
to remind them. Make me
a grocery bagger or a masseuse.

I am the wind chime and the music.
Why so quiet, music? Why so cold?
What is this tricky wrapping paper?

THE GENIUS HAS SEX

or tries to. She is rolling on top of him
and he is struggling simultaneously
to unhinge her bra and not swallow

her too soon. She is crawling
into his mouth with her tongue.
Her breasts look like small cakes

and he is cupping them, groping
a dark room for sharp edges.
She is moving her hips faster

and he needs to close his eyes
to stop himself from collapsing
the house of cards. From deflating

the tires. From melting every crayon
in the house. He imagines sad poems, hundreds
of gray hats turning black in the rain,

but she drags her hands down his chest
as if motioning the beginning of a race.
He opens his eyes and it is over.

The Genius Has Sex

They try again. This time
he moves quicker. He is inside her
before she is half-undressed.

The rocking begins, the quick
knocking of a stranger to be let in.
It is over soon and it does not remind

either of them of dreaming, of opening
your eyes after and it is all still real,
still breathing heavy beside you.

THE MICROPHONE
For Guante

The emcee does not make eye contact.
He raps facing the speakers. His left side,
his good side, in profile—a portrait

of a dead president. He grips
the microphone like a teenager
jerking off to his record cover.

He speaks to the beat, tells it
how to keep its shit together.
The audience is staring at him

but not really watching. The audience
is nodding their heads but they aren't smiling.
They aren't dancing or clapping or weeping;

they are just nodding their heads
and he is holding the microphone
not like a cock but like this is

the kind of pleasure that hurts.
Like this is the last thing his grandfather
said before unplugging himself.

Like this is the hottest pepper picked
from the vine with his teeth. He is hurting
himself for this. This is the chorus he woke up

choking on. This is the American dream:
to scream at the deaf. To sell your autobiography
for five dollars and a handshake.

This is the most romantic stroke.
His whole left side is numb,
just nodding their heads.

The Genius Considers the Pros and Cons of Pornography

It's not always pretty. I have seen

the botched surgery of sex,
the amputation. I have seen things

done with spoons I cannot unsee.

But all this mess, all this sweat and daddy
and fetish: this is the textbook of the body,

the instruction manual.

To exchange the gift for the cash.
To compose the jingle to fucking.

This is the dumb cousin of love making

who taught you to forget your table manners.
To eat with your fingers.

Prayer to the Saint of Leaving

Let us no longer wake up
sweating in a summer bed.

Let us never eat grapefruits
from each other's laps.

Let us stray quickly
into this Garden of Sleeping Alone.
This Garden of Heartache has found itself
a labyrinth inside me.

Let this be easy.
Let this be the last time
my heart is wrong.

Let his hands not surrender
up my thighs. Let him not
unwrap me. Let him
not find in me a new body
again and again.

Let him not love me.
Let it not be so.

The Genius Leads the Congregation in Prayer

Let us call the White House.

Let us lie down in the middle of a crowded
dance floor with our ears to the concrete.

Let us ask the dealer to Hit Me. Let us ask the dealer

to heal our mothers, to deliver unto us better jobs,
to crown us fertile enough to have a baby.

Let us beg for a better hand.

THE GENIUS DISCUSSES SUICIDE

To carve your name onto the trophy of the noose
and the floorless. To spit-shine it for eternity.

To become not why your father drinks, but what

carries him on a chariot of tremors
to drink again. To sign up for the obituary

circus: Come see the magical, the ones

who do what others cannot.
See the Exhaust Swallower.

The Dangling Acrobat. The Blue-Finned Mermaid

who floats face down in a tank
with gills on her wrists. To stare and be stared at

forever. The unsaid word. The forgotten

dream. The poem she will
always write and never finish.

ODE TO UNADILLA, NY

After Kevin Young

I want my homeroom
to be the same

as my parents'. I want

illegal fireworks
on the 4th of July

lit by the sheriff.
I want to skinny dip

in the Susquehanna River
behind the old folks' home.

I want to lose my virginity

in a tent. I want sidewalks
as crooked and broken

as teeth. I want venison,
cut from the deer

on my front porch.

I want hand-painted
business signs. Pete's Garage.

The Village Variety.

I want to always ride shotgun
in my father's pickup.

I want the trees

on Main Street to fold in
around us like the ceiling

of a chapel,
like he is walking me

down the aisle.

THE GENIUS CRIES

He imagined what would happen
if he let his bathtub overflow.

He pictured the ocean
that would fill his bathroom
and leak into the rest of his home.

The sea creatures that would squeeze
out of the faucet and into his living room.
The shells that would collect like cobwebs.
The seaweed clinging to his refrigerator.

He let himself cry.
Open. Gulping for air.
When nothing happened,

when no whale birthed itself
from his tear ducts, when
the downstairs neighbors
did not complain of flooding,

he realized he was not
the unnatural disaster he once was.
His pain was no longer something
one could drown in.

IV

THE GENIUS SWIMS THE ENGLISH CHANNEL

or THE GENIUS EATS AN ENTIRE TRACTOR
or THE GENIUS TELLS THE TRUTH
or THE GENIUS LIVES IN A CELLAR
FOR TWENTY-THREE YEARS

is the name of the autobiography he wrote last summer.
He has never done any of these things.

He hasn't even written the autobiography yet,
but he believes he can. He believes he can

tell her the truth one day. He will clear his throat
and straighten his bowtie and she will lean in

like a hungry bird. He will say YOU
DO NOT NEED TO SUFFER ANYMORE

and she will laugh and laugh and her hair
will bob up and down like an excited puppy.

Because suffering is the bible she was sworn in on.
Because self-doubt was the ferry she took to get here

and yes, it did get her here, but she never
knew she could swim.

After We Break Into My Apartment Because I Lost My Keys

We joke about what we would actually steal

if we were breaking in for reasons other than carelessness.
A nice quilt. A DVD player from the nineties.

Week-expired milk. I am rich, I tell you.

It has been a week since I've been in my apartment.
I want to touch everything. I want to wash every dish

in the kitchen sink like a newborn.

I want to pull you to the floor to make love
among the ticket stubs, the bobby pins,

the evidence of living.

Best Man

Inevitably, my father will cry at my wedding.

He will be dressed in his only suit coat
which he wears as naturally as a cardboard box.
His jeans, his tie mechanically hung like tinsel.

Not one for formal events, he tends to shift
in his seat, impatient as a handsaw.
When he cries—and he always cries

the way only a father of three women
does—his chest is a tired buoy. It sighs
and rises and everything in his face sinks

as if someone tossed a rock
into the pond. The ripples expand forever.
It is the most beautiful drowning.

The Genius Goes to the Barber

He was planning on growing his beard all summer.
He was planning on taking a bus to the Redwoods

and getting *I Am So Small* tattooed across his chest
in Gothic font like a banner or a for sale sign,

but his beard started catching things. At first,
it was just your typical crumbs, dribbles of soup.

One day, he found an entire angel
food cake entangled in his whiskers while

brushing his teeth. Then, darker things began finding
their home there, closer and closer to his mouth.

A nasty word someone called the garbage man.
The look a mother gave her child for spilling his juice.

A nightmare in which his entire life was a sitcom
and he kept forgetting his lines and the laugh track

kept rolling and rolling. It all clung to his chin
like icicles. They became so heavy;

he had no choice but to use them.
He didn't tip the server. He stopped cleaning

his fish tank. It wasn't until he found himself
screaming at a senior citizen WHY DON'T YOU

JUST HURRY UP AND DIE, YOU OLD WH—
when the barber rushed him into the shop, forced him

into the chair. *We only carry what we think we need,*
he said as he turned on the razor.

Reassurance to Sierra in High School

Don't worry. The acne will go away, sort of.
You will stop fighting with your sisters when they go
to college. This will be because of two things: your inability

to steal their clothing and the realization
that they are older, cooler versions of you. Your bully
will end up shaving her head and going to jail

or she will become a lawyer and have a nice car
and six babies. You will have no idea. You will forget
what she looks like, remember her the way

one remembers a splinter. You will stop
loving sharp things. You will learn how to make
your bed without being forced or threatened.

You will break up with your high school
sweetheart. I know, this is a surprise
but trust me. Yes, he loves you,

but it is a smothering love, the way
a dog nurses an open wound, all bared teeth
and tongues. When you leave him,

it will not feel like crushing a light bulb
in your hand—more like slowly, so slowly,
removing the glass from your palm.

For years after him, you will let your heart
hang open like a soup kitchen. This is not
a bad thing, more a lesson in proportions.

After graduation, you will change a hundred
times over, a revolving door, a waterfall.
One day, you will learn how to give

and receive love like an open window
and it will feel like summer every day.
One day, everything will make sense.

BALANCE

The state champion wrestler is in love.
His sweetheart is a quiet girl who wears flannel.
Because he is a wrestler, he understands balance,
what it takes to overpower another.

His sweetheart is a quiet girl. After high school,
they will marry and live on top of a hill.
He will not forget what it takes to overpower another;
he will discover his need to drink.

On the hill, he will build a house by hand
and she will grow a garden in the front yard.
He will begin collecting his anger in liquor bottles.
She will bury her voice in the dirt.

One day, she will discover she is growing a baby.
He will be at the bar when her water breaks and
she will wait in silence for two hours before he comes home
because they don't own a telephone.

On seeing his daughter, he will not go back to the bar.
The kitchen sink will become cluttered with baby bottles,
cloth diapers hung out to dry on the telephone pole.
One night, he will dream his daughter grown up,

emptying bottles of anger in the kitchen sink.
She is in love with a state champion wrestler.
She is the lead in a high school play about her mother.
She is an acrobat. She is learning to understand balance.

THE FIELD

Don't worry. Baseball practice has been out
for hours. In this town, children aren't allowed

out after dark and it is dusk. Walk to the center

of the diamond. Peel off the husk of your dress.
Sit down. Let first and third base guide your legs

away from each other, as simply as opening a pair

of scissors. The dugouts will drop their wooden jaws.
The dirt will roll over and blush beneath you. Spread the lips

of grass until you are buried, buried. You are the center

of the earth. You are what spins the record. You are
conducting this wild chain-link orchestra of heart. Touch

yourself. Do not think of anyone else.

THE GENIUS WRITES A LETTER

It began as an apology. By now,
Mistake's heavy carcass was rotting.
A cloud of flies began following him

around like bad weather every day
or an ugly balloon. As soon as he wrote
the words *I'm sorry*, Mistake got up

from the ground, brushed off its coat
and excused itself with the politeness of a butler.
He felt so much gratitude, the apology

became a thank-you letter. An I-owe-you-
so-much,-let-me-cook-for-you letter. An I-am-so-glad
neither-of-us-is-dead letter. And because

thankfulness is the kitchen floor of love,
he had no choice but to write out exact directions
to his heart I'm sorry I love you Don't
leave.

EVOLUTION IN NINE PARTS

I

My earliest memories of my mother
are sunburned. Pink cheeks,
Braids. Dirt under fingernails.

II

Before me, she was already self-conscious
about her stomach. Then I was made and I was too stubborn
to turn upside down inside her and they had to
cut her open and pull me out.

III

I learned how to put on lipstick
by watching her get ready for work
in the morning. I learned
how to criticize myself
by watching her cluck
at the mirror, swatting her hair
down like a bad dog.

IV

I am sorry for the white worm
I left across your middle.

V

She believes my sisters and I chose her
to be our mother. Handpicked her
from a basket of others.

This one. This one will teach us the most.

VI

Learn to cherish this vessel,

the tired music of the body.
To grow. To grow.

Let the skin be witness.

VII

I am standing in front of a mirror.
I am insulting myself out of habit and suddenly
my mother stops me, "Don't say that, Sierra.
If you think you are ugly, you are creating
that ugliness inside you."

VIII

I am thankful for the bed in your belly.
I was a weary traveler.

IX

My mother has a birthmark
the size of a grapefruit on her hip.
It is red and exploding.

I can only imagine
when she undressed for my father
the first time, it was like
watching the sun come up.

THE GENIUS FALLS ASLEEP IN CHURCH

As the preacher spoke, he waited for the warmth of God to draw itself over him like a bath. He even sang, loudly, hoping to catch some of Him in his mouth. The stained glass reminded him of the neon cereal he ate as a child. The tops of the ladies' hats made him feel as if he was sitting in the middle of an English garden. He closed his eyes and dreamed he was a butterfly. He was flying in the Garden of Eden. God was posing for the Sistine Chapel and let him land on His pointer finger and said, "You are the prettiest butterfly I've ever seen." His voice was higher than he had expected and he noticed He had long blonde hair and breasts and suddenly She was guiding him away from the garden, away from the pews, into a field of bluish grass. She stopped in front of a low-hanging cloud. "Kneel," She said, and he bent his four knees, because he was no longer a butterfly but a centaur and She placed the cloud on his head like a wreath of pillow stuffing. She kissed his forehead. A flower grew from the lipstick smudge. She held his cheeks as She said, "There are no gates to heaven. There are no doors to happiness. Go forth and love like a choir of mirrors. There is no collar on the beast of sadness, but it does not hunt for you. My darling, wake up. Wake up. It's morning."

ACKNOWLEDGEMENTS

Mom & Dad, thank you for your emotional encouragement and spiritual guidance. Thank you for living boldly. You inspire me to do the same. I love you.

Neil, thank you for making me write when I didn't want to, edit when I didn't want to, and talk about it when I didn't want to. You are an amazing person. Without you, this book would not exist.

Dylan, thank you for being nit-picky, critical, stubborn and hard to please. You are a great editor. Thank you for making me better.

Michael, thank you for teaching me almost everything I know about poetry, which isn't much.

Derrick, thank you for this gift, this amazing opportunity.

Daniel, Stevie, Gabrielle, & WB family, thanks for your support and inspiration.

Brian, thank you for letting me borrow your computer, on which I wrote this entire book.

Rya, *that's what I mint!*

The following poems have been previously published:

"The Perm," "Baptism," and "Best Man" – *Used Furniture Review*

"Reassurance to Sierra in High School," "The Microphone," and "Love, Forgive Me" – *The Legendary*

"The Genius Considers the Pros and Cons of Pornography" and "The Genius Shares His Opinion of Astrology" – *Muzzle Magazine*

"The Genius Visits the Psychic," "The Genius Leads the Congregation in Prayer," "The Genius Discusses Suicide," "The Genius Goes to the Barber," and "The Genius Falls Asleep in Church" – *Frigg*

"The Genius Goes to the Art Museum," "The Genius Has Sex," "The Genius Has Sex," and "Balance" – *PANK Magazine*

"The Genius Performs Taxidermy" and "The Genius Writes a Letter" – *kill author*

ABOUT THE AUTHOR

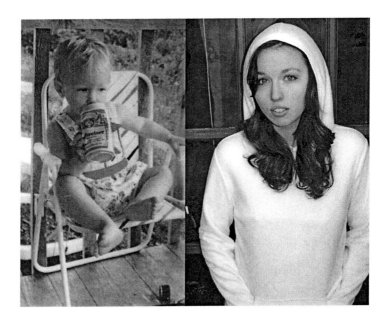

Sierra DeMulder lives in Saint Paul, MN. Her poems have been featured in numerous literary journals, including *PANK, kill author,* and *Muzzle Magazine.* In addition to being a two-time National Poetry Slam champion, Sierra has read her work in hundreds of venues across the country. While not performing poetry, she enjoys painting, cooking and waxing on and on about feminism. *New Shoes on a Dead Horse* is her second book.

NEW WRITE BLOODY BOOKS FOR 2012

Strange Light
The *New York Times* says, "There's something that happens when you read Derrick Brown, a rekindling of faith in the weird, hilarious, shocking, beautiful power of words." This is the final collection from Derrick Brown, one of America's top-selling and touring poets. Everything hilarious and stirring is illuminated. The power of *Strange Light* is waiting.

Who Farted Wrong? Illustrated Weight Loss For the Mind
Syd Butler (of the sweet band, Les Savvy Fav) creates sketchy morsels to whet your appetite for wrong, and it will be delicious. There is no need to read between the lines of this new style of flash thinking speed illustration in this hilarious new book. Why? There are not that many lines.

New Shoes on a Dead Horse
The Romans believed that an artist's inspiration came from a spirit, called a genius, that lived in the walls of the artist's home. This character appears throughout Sierra DeMulder's book, providing charming commentary and biting insight on the young author's creative process and emotional path.

Good Grief
Elegantly-wrought misadventures as a freshly-graduated Michigan transplant, Stevie Edwards stumbles over foal legs through Chicago and kneels down to confront the wreckage of her skinned knees.

After the Witch Hunt
Megan Falley showcases her fresh, lucid poetry with a refreshing lack of jaded undertones. Armed with both humor and a brazen darkness, each poem in this book is another swing of the pick axe in this young woman's tunnel, insistent upon light.

I Love Science!
Humorous and thought provoking, Shanney Jean Maney's book effortlessly combines subjects that have previously been thought too diverse to have anything in common. Science, poetry and Jeff Goldblum form covalent bonds that put the poetic fire underneath our bunsen burners. A Lab Tech of words, Maney turns language into curious, knowledge-hungry poetry. Foreword by Lynda Barry.

Time Bomb Snooze Alarm
Bucky Sinister, a veteran poet of the working class, layers his gritty truths with street punk humor. A menagerie of strange people and stranger moments that linger in the dark hallway of Sinister's life. Foreword by Randy Blythe of "Lamb of God".

News Clips and Ego Trips
A collection of helpful articles from *Next...* magazine, which gave birth to the Southern California and national poetry scene in the mid-'90s. It covers the growth of spoken word, page poetry and slam, with interviews and profiles of many poets and literary giants like Patricia Smith, Henry Rollins and Miranda July. Edited by G. Murray Thomas.

Slow Dance With Sasquatch
Jeremy Radin invites you into his private ballroom for a waltz through the forest at the center of life, where loneliness and longing seamlessly shift into imagination and humor.

The Smell of Good Mud
Queer parenting in conservative Oklahoma, Lauren Zuniga finds humor and beauty in this collection of new poems. This explores the grit and splendor of collective living, and other radical choices. It is a field guide to blisters and curtsies.

OTHER WRITE BLOODY BOOKS (2003 - 2011)

Great Balls of Flowers (2009)
Steve Abee's poetry is accessible, insightful, hilarious, compelling,
upsetting, and inspiring. TNB Book of the Year.

Everything Is Everything (2010)
The latest collection from poet Cristin O'Keefe Aptowicz,
filled with crack squirrels, fat presidents, and el Chupacabra.

Working Class Represent (2011)
A young poet humorously balances an office job with the life
of a touring performance poet in Cristin O'Keefe Aptowicz's third book of poetry

Oh, Terrible Youth (2011)
Cristin O'Keefe Aptowicz's plump collection commiserates and celebrates
all the wonder, terror, banality and comedy that is the long journey to adulthood.

Hot Teen Slut (2011)
Cristin O'Keefe Aptowicz's second book recounts stories of
a virgin poet who spent a year writing for the porn business.

Dear Future Boyfriend (2011)
Cristin O'Keefe Aptowicz's debut collection of poetry tackles
love and heartbreak with no-nonsense honesty and wit.

38 Bar Blues (2011)
C. R. Avery's second book, loaded with bar-stool musicality and brass-knuckle poetry.

Catacomb Confetti (2010)
Inspired by nameless Parisian skulls in the catacombs of France,
Catacomb Confetti assures Joshua Boyd's poetic immortality.

Born in the Year of the Butterfly Knife (2004)
The Derrick Brown poetry collection that birthed Write Bloody Publishing.
Sincere, twisted, and violently romantic.

I Love You Is Back (2006)
A poetry collection by Derrick Brown.
"One moment tender, funny, or romantic, the next, visceral, ironic,
and revelatory—Here is the full chaos of life." (Janet Fitch, *White Oleander*)

Scandalabra (2009)
Former paratrooper Derrick Brown releases a stunning collection of poems written
at sea and in Nashville, TN. About.com's book of the year for poetry.

Workin' Mime to Five (2011)
Dick Richards is a fired cruise ship pantomimist. You too can learn
his secret, creative pantomime moves. Humor by Derrick Brown.

Don't Smell the Floss (2009)
Award-winning writer Matty Byloos' first book of bizarre, absurd, and deliciously
perverse short stories puts your drunk uncle to shame.

Reasons to Leave the Slaughter (2011)
Ben Clark's book of poetry revels in youthful discovery from the heartland
and the balance between beauty and brutality.

Birthday Girl with Possum (2011)
Brendan Constantine's second book of poetry examines the invisible lines
between wonder & disappointment, ecstasy & crime, savagery & innocence.

The Bones Below (2010)
National Slam Champion Sierra DeMulder performs and teaches
with the release of her first book of hard-hitting, haunting poetry.

The Constant Velocity of Trains (2008)
The brain's left and right hemispheres collide in Lea Deschenes' Pushcart-Nominated
book of poetry about physics, relationships, and life's balancing acts.

Heavy Lead Birdsong (2008)
Award-winning academic poet Ryler Dustin releases his most
definitive collection of surreal love poetry.

Uncontrolled Experiments in Freedom (2008)
Boston underground art scene fixture Brian Ellis
becomes one of America's foremost narrative poetry performers.

Yesterday Won't Goodbye (2011)
Boston gutter punk Brian Ellis releases his second book of poetry,
filled with unbridled energy and vitality.

Write About an Empty Birdcage (2011)
Debut collection of poetry from Elaina M. Ellis that flirts with loss,
reveres appetite, and unzips identity.

Ceremony for the Choking Ghost (2010)
Slam legend Karen Finneyfrock's second book of poems ventures
into the humor and madness that surrounds familial loss.

Pole Dancing to Gospel Hymns (2008)
Andrea Gibson, a queer, award-winning poet who tours with Ani DiFranco,
releases a book of haunting, bold, nothing-but-the-truth ma'am poetry.

These Are the Breaks (2011)
Essays from one of hip-hops deftest public intellectuals, Idris Goodwin

Bring Down the Chandeliers (2011)
Tara Hardy, a working-class queer survivor of incest, turns sex,
trauma and forgiveness inside out in this collection of new poems.

City of Insomnia (2008)
Victor D. Infante's noir-like exploration of unsentimental truth and poetic exorcism.

The Last Time as We Are (2009)
A new collection of poems from Taylor Mali, the author
of "What Teachers Make," the most forwarded poem in the world.

In Search of Midnight: the Mike Mcgee Handbook of Awesome (2009)
Slam's geek champion/class clown Mike McGee on his search for midnight
through hilarious prose, poetry, anecdotes, and how-to lists.

1,000 Black Umbrellas (2011)
Daniel McGinn's first internationally released collection from 'everyone's favorite
unknown author' sings from the guts with the old school power of poetry.

Over the Anvil We Stretch (2008)
2-time poetry slam champ Anis Mojgani's first collection: a Pushcart-Nominated batch of backwood poetics, Southern myth, and rich imagery.

The Feather Room (2011)
Anis Mojgani's second collection of poetry explores storytelling and poetic form while traveling farther down the path of magic realism.

Animal Ballistics (2009)
Trading addiction and grief for empowerment and humor with her poetry, Sarah Morgan does it best.

Rise of the Trust Fall (2010)
Award-winning feminist poet Mindy Nettifee releases her second book of funny, daring, gorgeous, accessible poems.

Love in a Time of Robot Apocalypse (2011)
Latino-American poet David Perez releases his first book of incisive, arresting, and end-of-the-world-as-we-know-it poetry.

No More Poems About the Moon (2008)
A pixilated, poetic and joyful view of a hyper-sexualized, wholeheartedly confused, weird, and wild America with Michael Roberts.

The New Clean (2011)
Jon Sands' poetry redefines what it means to laugh, cry, mop it up and start again.

Miles of Hallelujah (2010)
Slam poet/pop-culture enthusiast Rob "Ratpack Slim" Sturma shows first collection of quirky, fantastic, romantic poetry.

Sunset at the Temple of Olives (2011)
Paul Suntup's unforgettable voice merges subversive surrealism and vivid grief in this debut collection of poetry.

Spiking the Sucker Punch (2009)
Nerd heartthrob, award-winning artist and performance poet, Robbie Q. Telfer stabs your sensitive parts with his wit-dagger.

Racing Hummingbirds (2010)
Poet/performer Jeanann Verlee releases an award-winning book of expertly crafted, startlingly honest, skin-kicking poems.

Live for a Living (2007)
Acclaimed performance poet Buddy Wakefield releases his second collection about healing and charging into life face first.

Gentleman Practice (2011)
Righteous Babe Records artist and 3-time International Poetry Champ Buddy Wakefield spins a nonfiction tale of a relay race to the light.

How to Seduce a White Boy in Ten Easy Steps (2011)
Debut collection for feminist, biracial poet Laura Yes Yes dazzles with its explorations into the politics and metaphysics of identity.

WRITE BLOODY ANTHOLOGIES

The Elephant Engine High Dive Revival (2009)
Our largest tour anthology ever! Features unpublished work by
Buddy Wakefield, Derrick Brown, Anis Mojgani and Shira Erlichman!

The Good Things About America (2009)
American poets team up with illustrators to recognize the beauty and wonder in our
nation. Various authors. Edited by Kevin Staniec and Derrick Brown

Junkyard Ghost Revival (2008)
Tour anthology of poets, teaming up for a journey of the US in a small van.
Heart-charging, socially active verse.

The Last American Valentine:
Illustrated Poems To Seduce And Destroy (2008)
Acclaimed authors including Jack Hirschman, Beau Sia, Jeffrey McDaniel,
Michael McClure, Mindy Nettifee and more. 24 authors and 12 illustrators
team up for a collection of non-sappy love poetry. Edited by Derrick Brown

Learn Then Burn (2010)
Exciting classroom-ready anthology for introducing new writers
to the powerful world of poetry. Edited by Tim Stafford and Derrick Brown.

Learn Then Burn Teacher's Manual (2010)
Tim Stafford and Molly Meacham's turn key classroom-safe guide
to accompany *Learn Then Burn*: A modern poetry anthology for the classroom.

Knocking at the Door: Poems for Approaching the Other (2011)
An exciting compilation of diverse authors that explores the concept of the Other
from all angles. Innovative writing from emerging and established poets.

WWW.WRITEBLOODY.COM

Pull Your Books Up
By Their Bootstraps

WRITEBLOODY
QUALITY AMERICAN BOOKS

Write Bloody Publishing distributes and promotes great books of fiction, poetry and art every year. We are an independent press dedicated to quality literature and book design, with an office in Long Beach, CA.

Our employees are authors and artists so we call ourselves a family. Our design team comes from all over America: modern painters, photographers and rock album designers create book covers we're proud to be judged by.

We publish and promote 8-12 tour-savvy authors per year. We are grass-roots, D.I.Y., bootstrap believers. Pull up a good book and join the family. Support independent authors, artists and presses.

Visit us online:

WRITEBLOODY.COM

CPSIA information can be obtained
at www.ICGtesting.com
Printed in the USA
FSOW02n2310121214
3817FS